A
Little
Middle
of the
Night

A Little Middle of the Night

Molly Brodak

UNIVERSITY OF IOWA PRESS, IOWA CITY

University of Iowa Press, Iowa City 52242
Copyright © 2010 by Molly Brodak
www.uiowapress.org
Printed in the United States of America

Design by Richard Hendel

The University of Iowa Press is a member of Green Press
Initiative and is committed to preserving natural resources.

Printed on acid-free paper

ISBN-13: 978-1-58729-858-5
ISBN-10: 1-58729-858-9
LCCN: 2009932828

For Nora, Pinnie,

and my teachers

O earthly animals, o minds obtuse!

The Primal Will, which of Itself is good,

from the Supreme Good—Its Self—never moved.

— Dante, *Paradiso, Canto XIX*

I give myself a second thought. Life is just forgetting

ahead like the carcass of a dead horse by the Niger Dam.

— J. A. Okeke Anyichie,

    Adventures of the Four Stars

Contents

(((

(((

Acknowledgments

Grateful acknowledgment is made to the editors of the publications in which the following poems first appeared:

"Niger Lullaby," *Colorado Review*; "Lake-like," *FIELD: Contemporary Poetry and Poetics*; "Roman Girls," *Hayden's Ferry Review*; "Like Your Jesus, Only Mine," the *Journal*; "Cabaret Voltaire" and "Les Blessures Graves," the *Laurel Review*; "Snow White," *Malahat Review*; "I HOPE YOU'RE HAPPY: A Novel," *Ninth Letter*; "Before Memory," *Northwest Review*; "Midwest Wilderness," *Sou'wester*; "Joseph Conrad's Last Novel (Which is Comprised Entirely of Face Colors from His Previous Novels)," *Washington Square*.

Some of these poems appeared in a limited-edition chapbook entitled *Instructions for a Painting* published in the Midwest Chapbook Series by GreenTower Press, 2007. Thank you to Mary Ann Samyn, Ed Haworth Hoeppner, Jeffrey Insko, Kathy Fagan, Dennis Allen, Marit Ericson, Mary Ruefle, Holly Carver, Matthew Porter, and to my family and friends for support.

A
Little
Middle
of the
Night

Niger Lullaby

Night comes,
icky baby,
born under the four coins—

on our reed raft,
even the good storm
moves off.

Every knife
you push in a man
will want out.

So the heart's room is black.
Listen, cloud curls, even
grackles bear a gold mouth:

they say *stay in dreams*
born on a sickbed,
o night beach—

bring your flame
under black burlap,
no matter what.

Poem for a Child's Voice

The first sound I hated came from the forest, so I went there.
I didn't wake up blindfolded. I didn't come to a door.
                    The moss was all

above me, half-lit, map damp.
I thought: it *will never be easier than now*.

Fought barely at first
against a steady massacre of clouds

in the arms of the pines, unashamedly
sharpened. Soon, trees were not tall enough—
                    their seeds rustled

like they owned the only longing,
& all the flaws that render a future.
Kept turning under and under every buried thing
until deep was not under but across.

To think I started with actual traps,
and the advice that my own notions were encoded:

instead, I found a trash heap, and train tracks. Heaps and heaps
of leads.

My live-in nurse says optimistic people will often see
brown as a shade of purple. *But the self implies a horizon,*

I don't say. She rouses me in order to change the bedclothes.
Just be thankful you have a breath to hold! Strange I have risen

at all, into this weird, white body, which I have not forgiven
for bruising up, freezing over, trying to leave me. Outside:

distance. The self is always on the horizon. How can I help it
if I look forward to a little loss. And actually, moonlight is warm,

yellowing—sunlight is bluish. Be careful of false clarity,
she says. *How little I need to breathe!* In three seconds

I will unfold and allow myself another blanket,
even if it brings nightmares: headless doves, singing.

Under Age

—under a crusted hair cascade I won't move for school photos.
I see this planet, ok: ticking insects blanketing an egg.
I ignore most everything.

I don't believe the film of me will survive anyway
so I just keep living it. Ever under teachers in their foul clothes,
a curdled joke in a locker, pinned by the dream of an English boy's
    torso.

Lives are too long. I'm tired of being half-formed and perverting
everyone. What haven't I tried? Pleats will go on without me, sweet
sucky knee-socks and lavender blubber about the mouth. I was born

on a bad raft, thanks; I'll loom where my power creeps out.
I'll enact me a black boyfriend and find my fringes
under the weekend. Next century, up my skirt. Once I was a sponge,
now neon, lunatic.

And How Did Your Rapture Turn Out?

Once I
woke up laughing.

Saw the limbs of the pine
row and paw. I heard bells, split geologic.

Did anyone take a photo of me
while I was in the coma? Why, no. No one thought to.

Before, the nights froze in acid orange
streetlight, and we walked in thin shadows.

That was the first time I felt young.
There was no future.

But I came out on the other side—so
your millennium wasn't like mine,

so what. Remember catching that wet rabbit?
How did it feel. Like dusk—

start at the stars and drop west & the light goes apocalyptic:
indigo, ultramarine, cobalt, turquoise, cerulean.

I said *come watch the bats with me,*
once. I just kept up.
That's how.

Before Memory

As an infant, my eyes
wouldn't stay—

only ever looked up.
       Good as lakes

for lenses, good as pennies.
I'm not supposed to remember this.

In flashbulbs
they went owlish,
lacquered in oil blue.

(((

They said I had a cold shore,
I think, a cold shore.
I had to hope myself open.

You wouldn't think from looking.

(((

Then, winter:
       a little milk, a little vinegar.

Yes, it was suddenly one day—
my mother was humming,

her fingers
were in my hair, and
       from the window—
       an ice blink,

a bite behind my eyes and the light came in.
My tooth throbbed like a bell
in the brightening.

I had on a dress from here to there.

(((

First, I saw the pink string lights
wound around the elm trunk and limbs,
just a few freakish bends illuminated.

Then a December sky—mostly darkness,
or the color of *far-off*. The furs
of someone carrying me to the car.

(((

       Now, a frozen river,
a mass of netted burr-reed and larch
         frosted over stiff,
         trash in the barbwire:

ridiculous, ridiculous. I began to know
how I am not a miracle.

(((

       This is not the beginning, this is not
YOU'VE GOT TO GO DOWN TO GO UP.

In other words,
      I began
      with a hand in a hand.

With a *he said really I just want a dance.*

Les Blessures Graves

My blood type is:
paper white,
a trill warble,
a new leaf.
The nurse
cuts my clothes off.

Enfin, my arms:
swing unhinged,
go soft like peaches,
can't hold a needle.
You won't be
expected:

to remember, or
to sign here.
The nurse can catch
those gauzy cottonwood
seeds for you—don't move so.
She asks:
what shall I wish?

The Horse Museum

—may've started way back at dust. Lost lines shown in the bones—
the toedip that spun off whales, wholly hoped for new food, and

these ever bellicose forelimbs, clawed even! So I adopted one or
   two, just
for a plaque for heaven's sake, as my coma

was just someone telling me it happened.
As a plane crashsite: seat here, seat there. Where'll

the eye rise? A long socket says *keep going*.
The brain feels nothing, supposedly; the heart begs for out.

I know to ask for a .22 gauge and offer the arm
I need least, but still the veins roll off or collapse.

*I want to say have I screamed? How long have I
been here?* Instead: *well . . . define hurt.* Because I can't tell

if I'm dull to it or if it is just everywhere. Then, nestless
waiting. Ordinarily I am ready for myself, but now, days

are just spans. So I snuck my chart. The tumor is slow—
many millimeters, scallop-edged! Imagine: some people

do not want to live. Some things push against it,
out of room. For family history I said *none*

and she wrote *neon.* Like the pit of my elbow
which has turned yellow. I tell myself to love

a color that can't be divided, like yellow. Such colors
will become desaturated and I won't know it.

The peripheral is already grey—soon gone. I wished
for a two-way mirror once, terrified at the doctor's

feverish touch, although ordinarily I hope for windows.
He said *there'll be no space left in your skull!* and I

felt guilty. I think of a bone door, a brain which *cannot
afford.* Nearby a coloring book also waits.

Everything running has that cartoon shoe—bread loaf,
flat-football (what foot that would fit!)—and doughnut

of sock. Such shape will tell you instantly how to treat it.
People also do this. The plate carries a girlspoon

(eyelashes tell) so she does not get the shoes, does not
need feet. And he doesn't look where he's going, but at her.

Or that is where he is going. Most things are held in
by their alleged colors, but not them. Ordinarily, a black line

won't make a space. I should revise my desires.
Also, gloves are everywhere. Except on the girlspoon

who doesn't have hands. A fly lands on the exam table
where I refuse to sit. I wonder if it is dark enough for stars yet.

Underneath Underneath

I get two books: one for the bedspread, one for me.

One from a Detroit warehouse with a receipt from St. Mark's.

One with a page once bent, now I cannot tell which direction.

The crease is just a *once*. Somebody's want, passed over.

A page as just an in-between.

Underneath, always, the soil that brightens and darkens.
So at first it was just soil.

I have been furious. I have been looking for an underneath
   I couldn't see.
With remote qualities.

A Good underneath will tell you to go back. You should feel
   lucky when you hear this.

A Private underneath will look like everyone else's.

A Faithful underneath will be the one you dislike first.

(The wisdom I have heretofore trusted was cowardice, the leaper.)

Likewise, mine is an acid-green leafshoot. Talk about underneath!
Talk about neglect.

Underneath at All

Mirror is a limited response. Stupid sympathy.
Attention is tidal. Like:

what's with you wearing your shoes in the house all of a sudden?

Then, pulls inward. Jealous of the thicket with all the birds.

That kind of underneath isn't beckoning from anywhere; it is
    beckoning.
Upstairs, I had time to think about art:

which should've stopped at Baroque. Meaning, an earthy
    obsession with entrails.
That dovetails with General Nameless Unease. Because the
    puffery was accurate, at least,

and the future had scalloped edges.

Such archeology says how *neatly silence describes the thing.*

The underneath says stop looking for an edge. And how.
I would wish for a house-sized instrument, a walk-in camera.

Underneath (Side Effects)

We play the Make This Shape into Something game and he says
you always draw the same shape. It grows worse, like a body.

Similarly, I like "heaven forbid" but it means nothing to me. That
    doesn't mean
there is nothing underneath. That doesn't mean the underneath
    is full of me.

A small part of what I've seen has lead me to believe this.
Including the fake things. Mostly I believe there is no me.
    So, listen,

I'm afraid of where I will go under the anesthesia. Don't think
belief is uninterruptible. *There is a reason, then there is murder,*
    forgetfulness.

Normal and not normal. In my dream, Mom brings me a tassel
    of robin's feet.
I have an owl in a cage exactly the size of its body. It escapes
    just moments later.

Underneath

Ever to admit my loneliness is unnecessary
and hedge in whatever frail danger is left in me

doesn't explain why things feel so inside out.

The last dump and trailer on the edge of town—
which way to the wilderness? Which edge.

Let them think
we need to witness our own limits transgressed.

Let them think there are limits.

I was the littlest wastebasket.
I was my own church. Except—
scared, scared.

5/13/06
Watching "Surviving the Icelandic Sea"—

> *The ship is also the processor.*
> *There is a trough for spines, dumps to the ocean*

when he walks in the room like read it and weep.
Somehow, I deserve this.
The man who swam on his back for two days

> *spoke to myself. Spoke to the gulls.*

Pulled his body to a shore of lava fields. No one believed him.

> *They kept*
> *putting me back in.*

> *All my life, for research.*

Why have you not given up on us?

> *80 minutes in ice water*
> *did not explain it.*

5/19/06
Quakes in 1811 changed the course of the Mississippi—
I've also felt landless, cloudless—
in bed when the sparrows suddenly cease.
Noticed the north light seemed more horizontal, accosting.

5/21/06
A Melville novel, as abridged by me:

But as for their fingers, they were enveloped in some myth.
"Looks are one thing, and facts are another!"

"Brightening?"
Brightening it may be, but less like the white of an egg in coffee,
than like the stove-lustre on a stove—black, brightening.
It is past finding out.

The boat touched at a houseless landing, scooped, as by land-slide,
out of somber forests;

"Go, bone-set the crooked world, and then come bone-set crooked me."

The End.

7/22/06
Then, another sea:
virtual, as they say.

D. in her kitchen
was a tight ship—
a puff of dandelion in lucite.

Imagine not caring
like that. Can I choose?

Today this hunger, this jealous eyegloss
—inky, sorryless!—
came to beat down my door.
Their poems are fine but I don't want fine.

Meanwhile,
        crashing.
I've decided to fight and here's why.

12/1/06
I moved rooms again;
I sleep in no one's bed.

The bellmen know the handsome sadness
is a hotel. They can't be surprised.

Found books
in the nightstand:
What Business Should I Start?
Why Men Marry Some Women and Not Others

Evil is Not Your Enemy
What Do People Do All Day

Most of this
is How To.

Here's a book:
Your Life
is Going Off.

Here's a book:
Wake the Fuck Up.

12/24/06
~~I wasn't myself~~. Why would I close my good eye?
These still-life things become the back of death.
The lilies he has sent. This is the peel away part.

We want the Exact and the Vast;

we want our Dreams and our Mathematics . . .

— R. W. Emerson

Mild Peril

I might find a blueblack sky when I'm ready
to feel all the moments, not just the sleazy important ones.

To uncoil the wild little everything
inside this *now*, which I am crouching to fit into.
Three forty-seven a.m. in the dooryard.

Providence. Resolve. ~~Alcohol~~.
I am afraid of my dreams.

Maybe a mourning dove wheezes out of a hedge,
lungs throbbed by its own wings

(they build
  bad nests

                              eggs often
                               slip out)

stupid and faithful. I left fondness up to you.
And now, we'll burn that bridge when we come to it.

I asked what is going to happen and he said *it's happening*.

Going Back to Sleep

A minute ago, a whistle or laugh
from a flabby tree. A ring of chintz girls,
clasped around the lidless corpse
I saw near Tigers Stadium. Dead bum,

dead for days, on my way to work. No thanks
clocks, or chore of pants. The day is to hate or laugh
or nothing: pick the least sick. I'm going back
                    to the blanket bucket. To the yellowy out.

i. *Gold Winter.*

I seem to remember your black eyes, see,
it would be fine if I never know you.

      Two straps on the back of a truck
go after me like arms. As splendor
is too often soft.

ii. *Tired of Designing Cereal Boxes.*

A year goes by and there you are.
The man in the next car says don't take me to the hospital.
      Goddamn most everything, goddamn us

right up the middle—
aches of teeth and the hate spot
in my chest; I saw it my way
and died there.

iii. *Understand:*

I listened to your recording.
There was a bird on Your End
or mine, that's all I thought about.
That and *The flood boiled with blood—the folk gazed on—*
and hot gore.

The black of the back of the trees against a lowland ombre.

iv. *Thinly Veiled.*

I didn't tell you, when my dad was in jail,
I went to see him once. A photo was taken

and I remember the cheery forest backdrop.
There were guards, vending machines, just like school.
Could you tell I had something to say? I would have given in.

Mulligan's golf dome—
among papier-mâché mountains,

pools and flows of hot blue
water foam white at the traps.

Limey plastic bottles are caught
in the eddies, caught and tumbling

all day. The water holds them,
somewhat rejects them.

Most boys stop on the bridge—
some lean over the blackened rope

and with mini-clubs, they fish
for a wrapper, or maybe nothing.

Lake Superior

I.

One warm shallow; a cobweb of sunlight
waves *hi, make yourself under* in icemelt,
this mercury channel. I find my hands

upon themselves, enormous
in the sea-like rock of the seiche,
chilly as butcher birds in the deep pine shade.
A spine goes sick from the burning blue sky into this,
bear brain gloom among sunshine.

II.

Plates of ice seemed fun at the time.
A dropped purple glove, pointing all directions at once.
A fake African necklace, the leaf of a fishbody, left.

Nothing lives sometimes, said mom,
but guard yourself from vague beliefs about it.
I stuck by the bone-white lighthouse,
while she went as farther than I could see.

Now she shouts:
fur comes   from
cold shores,

     following   rivulets,
stars   north   stars, flowers.

III.

Dumb lighthouse, I would have thought. Empty
sweet junk to those who are pleased by old tools.
Oh sure, you could run up the steps and back—

the light was blinding, glacial. Cottonwood seeds, one week,
trailed into drifts of puffs and did not melt; caught in the new
    erosion.
A man suddenly scooped up a dead wren with a playing card
and it was too far to hear what he said, or if he laughed when
    he threw it.

IV.

Michigan,
she said, *is an enormous black coat. Good luck*
with that. We watched trees toss juncos onto the parking lot.
When she was my age, she walked North one February
and built an igloo of blankets in dad's cabin and slept
for a week. Woke to the knock of a state trooper—
The one she stabbed; the one who dragged her back.

V.

The brass smell of Ontario wind and blood on a mitten—
whoops a nosebleed said mom and I let it rush into the snow crust.
Had I been her. Could I have tricked my every child or just this one.

That season an ice skater found the wreck of the *City of Winnipeg*—
dark and clear, just under, cradled in the fossils of a cedar forest.

VI.

I had a dream about the last rabbi in my family;
we were pushed up a spiral staircase. He said *I'm going to leave you*
    forever,
but I'll always move to any town you move to,

and I'll be wearing different clothes, and you may not know
that you are talking to me. *Look.* I woke up and wept,
walked to the dock in Mom's coat and the ice points of stars
shook the lakebottom some.

Appalachia

There is me and one of every bird.
Hay on the graves.

      Wet licks of an animal on my ankle, oh say
it's a good thing.   Take us out of here.

Wars begin inside of one person, imagine that.

We lived on borders: range to basin, plain to shore,
      a flood under the flood.

      One ripple against the coast became a deer,
three deer, huge on junk food. At quarter to four a.m.

I watch them climb the slope of our frontyard,
         one gallops up the steps.

North of North

In the lobby of a theater you dialed me—
clinks of a pinball in the background. Trouble

begins in distances. We know enough to keep going. Mountains
there had been topped to hold malls; the old peaks pushed

into a secret valley. Silence in the air beside the sound.
    Hideous streetlight
burns permanently against these black ravines—deer and crows
    crowd

at the edge of the cleared lot behind us. What's above
our old errors, and above those coldest places? Out of the bogs

of our wide glacial plain, an earth marked by retreat & enormous
inland seas who capture and recapture, a lower air transferred

our images: even without us. As breathing is forgettable.
I felt a sound when you called—a yellow bruise clouded across

my inner upper arm. In polar regions, yellow light carries
    farthest.
As the signal itself replies to the sender, having sent.

Dad thought he'd get shot.

Dye pack, red red red.

You remember,

how embarrassing he was.

Can I plead

insanity, he said.

One world: Poland,

in ho-hum infant Dad,

Vietnam black in his ribs,

& twilight Detroit for brains,

empty in empty. Money-

stung, bummer daughters:

he held out.

Built pressboard desks

in jail. Eight years, etc.

A serious chime

from some casino

lit an old light,

and he fought us,

fought cops, gave up

for cash—

a flux what seeks

the dark,

as a murmur of words,

come tumbling.

Released, he seemed old,

not good-old, not mean-old,

we joked. He knew

the way back,

fake gun, new note,

mystery especially:

at hand, mystery,

in the parking lot

at a party store, mystery.

A Little Middle of the Night

Somewhere a pipe organ plays the oldest, lowest sound from a
    fifty-foot pipe—
as a sound is only a span of time, as a key is also a lock. Also

here I am! I used to think. Lately, there is spangled shade in my
    space
and a cold apple orchard to tend in place of consciousness.

It isn't enough to be known. Or sad at heart
at the *thanks for the arrangement*: jumbo mums, cheap and
    sharp—

whose droop reminds me I'm in charge, good god, but not
    enough to stop
the accidents and the accidents of these mortarless weeks;

so tonight I stay in glasses, read *gait* as *guilt*, of course or
    sure enough.
I'm sorry for what I have always done. It still will happen.

Whoever Said Hell Is Not Beautiful

The doorknob was not hot.

If death meant

framelessness in landscape,

then I must've closed my eyes

at the next alarming vista—

moving towards the gigantic

until I became as small as I needed.

I felt for the edge

& left everyone.

The devil was a man taking bets

while his wife lived alone in bed.

Their trees grew aggressive

on the grade. We shouldered through

the abandoned bodies, made of crime—

bent to fan the gill of a fetus.

He said we couldn't be human

until we grew something *opposable*.

Down here you can walk way back

to that black vent in a Cambrian sea

and the thing at the lip

that wanted and tried.

I HOPE YOU'RE HAPPY A Novel

1: IN WHICH THE MAN SPEAKS FOR HIMSELF.

But when I said *this is a rare girl*
I meant like raw. It's not a dream.

2: A PATERNAL CONCERN.

Dear son,
I waited on the hill between an S of white mares
and a hot green Mountain Dew bottle, hard grass stubble
against my legs, reading, waiting, and you brought me her
only photo and she was making dirty eyes

3: IN WHICH THE GIRL DISCLOSES.

The history of our last night:

You don't know my eyes are open.
Sixteen minutes later I am in a weird court,

my calf is against your shin as we sleep.
What if I have a bat for a heart?

So I grew pines there and haunted them
with owls. That was me 136 years ago.

At seven we are asleep while downstairs
someone complains of *person-shaped lights.*

Outside, horses.
There is no new night.

4: ALSO ILLUMINATING.

My brother circles the pond at night,
and the stars give him bad counsel:

>   *don't go too far*

and

>   *measure, measure!*

he listens further—

past jellyfish of heart,
            blood's fireworks,
for:

there must be something better than happiness.

5: HE BLASPHEMES.

A word like *eternity*
says the very history of sadness.

The blackness that turns up lies
from the dirt and bile, the rummage

and stinking blood of a bombed hotel
and we all looked at each other and said God, ok—

*but as for their fingers, they were enveloped
in some myth*

6: WHICH IS RATHER CONCISE.

Promise of promise.

7: LOVELORN IN GREEN SILK.

Most of the world is the floor of the sea.
A worm can sweep its skirts of skin
and into the dark, remain dark in the motion.
This is not so far. Look at the eye

of an ape, a dog: looks enough like me.
But try: fish. Lobe-fin, bone of coelacanth.
Try new bodies for new lives.
I'd make a fine suit of love and disappear.

8: IN WHICH THEY MEMORIZE.

The crooked tooth who went first.

The way something blew your scarf
as you ran, tossing off *musts*.

The tyranny of dawn, repeating.

The snow-like window between us.

The shouldering through.

The cardinal that flew from a wound.

The spill of your hair-thin chain
as it broke while we slept

and the gold links became us,
and the locket was swallowed.

Pale Yellow Throat

1790

An end of things and it's all lit:

the bird's skeletal feet in a fortune
of jewel green scrub. I fell asleep at the end of land

because   let it rot

and I pushed my dream arms
into this picture plane.

While my real body slept in the car,
crossing the skirts of the mountain.

Held under little claws.

Changing my mind.

Green and pink light knitted across us; it was just a thought.
Bouquet of overrated roses on my real lap.

"Ha, ha. It will be warmer when

I blow the trumpet (if indeed

I ever do; for you are men,

And rest eternal sorely need)."

— Hardy, "Channel Firing"

Lake-like

Paint the sumac
chest-high, aching
out of somewhere
primitive.

Use blue only in a wild
spray of starlings
to tangle the pocket
of nothing above the highway.

Below, in the panic-grass and sedges
some dirty cat with the fur of its neck
knifed up—the same beige.

Leave dawn an indeterminate pink,
leave the cat with a cloud
for a mouth.

Make this whole hovering
over the yellow scrub
of lakeshore near Luna Pier—

it should belong to *your* hands.
It should already be old.

Lacan as an Australian Settler

There are stars here
but not enough.

What do I do with what I wanted?

Thought I carried my grid of money—
                    (unmappable me!)

Until I landed

and met everything other. Day one & some odd femur
defies England. And the interior sea is missing

—no,

pasture, pasture: another abandoned room

for my counterfeit emergence, capture—

my lonely little *a*? The frontier slides back
daily. See how long such need stays nameless

once we print new money. Let's say:
the queen, and more stars than ever,

in novel pigments, unthinkable engraving.
        Not these smug rocks.
        Not the poverty of the cloudless sky.

Distant anger clouds together.
As terrified ones tend to do.

The *after*, the vacuum—
the heat of imperceptible sadness
is gone before it's known.

So Jupiter lugs comets to and from
the sun and a woman in Managua
fires a gun into the sky.

Somewhere, belly-white,
a plume of dust replaces a building,
like some unintelligible word.

Still. A chime, a blush of
with what waste shall we rebuild
approaches. All is waste.

Cabaret Voltaire

Ball paid the balalaika orchestra
to play Romanian folk—*we shall do great things,*

he said, *play fast.*

> Across the street, Lenin
> heard *stupendous negro music* while writing.

(((

There were poems in all the coats.

> *the fun becomes confused*

shouts: let's destroy the organ! What's inside? What's inside?

(((

The first dance was Flycatching: clumsy, shrill, golden cut-out
hands—end in a pile.

Second dance: Cauchemar: stooping, arms lengthened by tubes,
try to laugh.

Third: Festive Desperation.

(((

So Lenin planned for bombs. Allowed for elimination dances.
> *The paralyzing horror which is the backcloth of our age is here
> made visible.*

So we stopped making up stories of how our horror was salvation
and just lived it.

(((

While Russolo made the organ sound like traffic.
>What instrument is the descendant of a weapon, he said.
>Is this a joke?

Arp's faithless reliefs bore down on us from the walls like no art
in history, *upon which we spat*

>as if heaven stank
more than our malty flesh and this dance floor, crumbling.

>Something must be stretched, beaten or pierced—
>you'll find sound in the wound! he said.

>We all laughed.

Those strolling through the Niederdorf found us easy to diagnose
and were not puzzled.

(((

When we unassembled the world, it disappeared:

Like Your Jesus, Only Mine

Wait up, bitch! begs back the pale bus stop boy.
O molester moustache, O fake hobble—
they group up—legs of toddler proportion, whatever glamour wants,
and papery shirts, long as dresses

hung with tangles of gold—
the kind that rubs off, once finger-loved.

Takes down his headphones. This white soul—too careful.
Crystal earrings sag sad like daffodil corollas—
their hollow stems knee-bent—trod over in campus beds of mud.
Tugs his hollow crotch, punches

the other boy's bony chest with his cell—still
pocket hot.
A darling lick of flame in there

stretches to the waitress bouncing—
her cheery muffin-top belly
above the tight jeans white-streaked down like a bone print.

He strips buds from the forsythia and settles
into the dim between.
Thinks this is what the darkness is for. However much.

Glitter of lip sweat when dad calls
—says *Yeah what's up.*
Inside—I don't care if I do.

There was no dancing then, either. The difficulty
was similar. But

no neon, gasoline, ice cubes. Buttons to push and
glasses to see

were surely dreamed of. No: it was easier.
Our shadows

simply made us more. Our cheeks went hot in sunlight:
no rouge. Boys

wore no hats—they would cut their fresh leather
sandal strings

with pearl-colored teeth, unbleached. It was more
than fashion.

And we could walk anywhere. The world was
small enough

to sing to in all directions. And maybe it is, again.
We'd sing *death*,

give us back our hearts, laughing, *they are all
we are*

Drawer of Cardinals

Cotton in eyesockets,
in beaks, in brain barns,
up the songbox, even so,
your curled claws
clutch to each other, to this hull
between emptinesses.
Wake, babies.

We need you back, cherrywings,
black chins, feeder bossies,
with your dun girls paired to you still;
grandma Barbara
found you funny.
Here's how wild ones
come to know an *inside*.
There is nothing in this world

not natural, loves, your honeycomb bones,
freakish quills, or leg tags, answerless.
Oh whole world, we choose
another.

What weird trees
would you've matched anyway?
We go dumb with easy eyes

upon your ruffled edge, sharp margins.
From some packed cavity they say *nope*,
you go.

Vermeer Sounds

Recent X-rays of *View of Delft* reveal:
compression of the rooftops, lazily,
a city reduced to its profile.

Yellow more dizzying, stained arms
of figures. Perhaps the use of a razor.
A sky ache above the Rotterdam gate.

A more accurate shoreline between them.
The dog, painted out, then dog again, then not.
The market's clatter and stink—

ruining the built-in grainy sentiment.
Which left those basket songs blank,
crystallized near the mouths of work.

A glint in the bell tower: better empty.
The half of hand under the sand—
any discernible breathing.

Things not painted at all:
the actual living blue figure.
Glittering whatsoever.

Cannons being cast
in the Armamentarium.
All their dull circumstance.

Snow White

> Some of them seem to be a kind of wilderness
> unto themselves.
>> —M. Robinson

1.

Wellside, the girl is a surface—
a trick of pigment

with a beetle gloss
for each eye, a little coal

and a saltless skin of pink
in perfect *rags*.

So why this box
for a bloodless heart?

2.

The *faithful huntsman*
offers his knife to her cheek

like a bright joke. She sees
her skin across the thin blade

and turns on its edge. Then a fall:
brambles and brambles.

With her cape and nothing—
bare-handed and no pockets for later.

Such illuminated animals catch her,
their wild eyes on her fingertips,

and the watercolored cloud
of animals and girl are hastened

in the same round wind, a stampede:
breathless, bright leading the bright.

3.
A creep of water,
then a hungry house of men

with their axes
and their diamonds—

another sharpened thing.
They ask can she make *apple dumplings*

and soon every door is a basket
of flame red apples, thousands

to choose. She thinks: if *snow*,
then perhaps ice, perhaps bones

are frozen wells. Perhaps a rosy
dawn is enough—something worth

softening for. The hunch of vultures
in the thrall of her wake

is like a black laugh
across those gaudy clouds.

4.

The men *fashion a casket*
of glass and gold

and don't ask anything.
Her whiteness is no longer a margin

but a new endlessness. They
arrange her hands, as always —

and find the weight of one apple
is the gravity of wanting, or weaponry.

Joseph Conrad's Last Novel (Which Is Comprised Entirely of Face Colors Used in His Previous Novels)

Cinnamon, Nut Brown, Yellow, Lemon Yellow,
Fatty Yellow, Shiny Yellow, Healthy Creole White
Which is Never Tanned by its Native Sunshine,
Clear, Twice as Sunbaked as Before, Shabby Gold,
Thinly Blue, Off-Black, of Too Much Swedish Punch,
Cooling Silver, Negrish, White as the Snows of Higuerota,
of Half-Raw Beef, of Rippling Copper, Semi-Translucent,
Waxy, Brick Dusty, of Quivering Leather, of Wet Hair,
Refreshingly Green, Poisonously Green, of Sodden Lead,
Dazzling Like a Ballroom with an Earthen Floor,
Invisibly Coloured, of Horn Powder, of a Hopeless Bird,
Besmeared with Tobacco, Exceedingly Rusted, of Crumbs,
Cigaresque, Betrayingly Pink, of Varied Loathsome Colors.

The Greek Theater

We come up

airless in the tall pines,
straight and away.

Embarrassed for the cheery blue
port-a-johns shouldering out
from behind a column.

The reflecting pool has grown soft inside,
billowed with muck but lifeless. Above,
Persephone holds her horns

as if to say: so. Brushed and trembling,
the pines keep the sky off of us—
still, she's bent with *the something*
of bronzes, maybe the inward
the pull of a hollow.

The First Poem

Now, get up—
that horizon circle
is edgeless, unstoppable.

But try.
Start with a window,
any edible box.

See what you
will fit through.
Your first poem

must have been
about this crown of pines,
the cirrus clouds far off,
and the wind between them.

The first poem:
wasn't a gold ring, or
a handkerchief trick.

It didn't
ask you to sit.

Ramp of the Chinese Dog

In an open elbow of marble
the dog has been rubbed faceless:
back into its first nature.
Unsharpened, invisible.

The cloud of ivy snaps in waves
after each wind on the dark wall—
a grackle with french fry
stops to look and loses half.

On the peristyle, visitors raise
their arms, dripping with bags
and purses, lazy from the wait
to point cameras, *take nothing*.

And their tired hearts knock
against the long-limbed bronzes
in the fountain like new moths.
The water reaches after them

in weird sprays, endlessly.
They think: then we must be nothing
if not broken. What's touchable
is underneath—

beyond our own dumb fingerprints
on the plexi. *Give us this. Surely
we've come at least this far.*

Lost, soundless in their soft shoes,
the families break around the dog
like water—down each heavy step,
wanting their cars.

Scene from an Unknown Painting

And along came the grail with two neutral angels.
Landscape crusted with thunder: it wasn't ready.

A black animal at pond's edge gathered the rustlings—
waves came, but not the kind you would think.

That was the primitive mistake. Which is still spinning off
the sleeve-tug of the present, and the future's gaping hope,

and what *spinning* means. Also: finger bones. Also tiny wings.
Also cat feet, birth moms, dead guns, make ups, left outs.

I saw the angels embarrassed of the swamp. Blushed at each other,
like animals, blushed at the weird trills, the rot on the wind.

Midwest Wilderness

Over the interior sea a field grew,
patchy snake grass, cold path:

drowsy quartz gravel muttered some,
warned me against the bad old future

as the sky cooled behind the elms
& the dogs went jewely eyed, rubyish, sapphiric.

I met a former friend at some distance:
she put on her hat like *if you're different*

then I am too. I forgot her lake-wave hair,
and frowned out *I'm not lonely either.*

While wind burned from the inside
and cats weaved around, homelessly,

I saw or thought I saw,
which is the same thing,

outer space, only a few miles away,
close and vast, spreading apart,

in the arbitrary palette of Uccello:
those corals, olive, aquamarine, chrome,

ecstasy in any direction. Black self, white self
lead the way into clouds stony & unreal—

a mourning dove blinked a sky blue eyelid
over the black pupil, the good wound.

And then you'll go back to bed for a long time.
Night black cat and books pin you in.

Yes there's the warning, then the forest,
but what about the coming back from that?

            What kind of—
—gate? Knife?

       The thing that followed me back: one crow, calling
suff-ring. Hope for pink light in the cracks. Just one other person.
Quarry for the gems and the darkness they come from.

One night there'll be doors where they weren't before.
       The cat kicks. When everyone else is gone,

there's a kind of jail, and there's music
for a moment. If you start to cry, go back to the beginning.
You may already know the last living person.

Because there was a need, you
       were fastened to the field of time.

Look,
trees still live deep in the city, in our buildings, our nervous
systems. The first story you'll hear is
         oh you've arrived too late! Hurry, join—

Real World Magic

Doves preen in an alcove of matted oak
and the day goes blue. I stood, memorizing,
memorizing. I thought I had been awake—

I had hoped. The mind is a half life,
then, none. What's worse? A snap of violet
lightning and *unharm me!* I said and awoke—

back into the beast, the dulled ache, dumb junk
clotted about the bed. For a weird while I sensed myself
formless in force, disarmed by a little sun, waking.

"The Underneath Suite": All italicized phrases and words are from Jorie Graham's books *Never* (HarperCollins, 2002) and *Swarm* (Ecco, 2000).

"Diary of a Year without Pictures": Quotes are from Herman Melville's *The Confidence-Man: His Masquerade* (W. W. Norton & Co., 2006).

"Mars Black": The italicized sentence is from *Beowulf*, translated by R. M. Liuzza (Broadview, 2000).

"Pale Yellow Throat": This poem is about a watercolor of the same name by the naturalist John Abbot, owned by the Morris Museum of Art in Augusta, Georgia.

"Lake-like": The form of this poem was inspired by Yoko Ono's book *Grapefruit* (Simon and Schuster, 1977) and is dedicated to her.

"Cabaret Voltaire": The italicized portions were borrowed from Hugo Ball's published diaries and Dadaist manifestos.

"The Greek Theater" and "Ramp of the Chinese Dog": These poems are named after places on the grounds of Cranbook Art Museum in Bloomfield Hills, Michigan.

"Scene from an Unknown Painting": This poem is based on Wolfram von Eschenbach's interpretation in *Parzival* of the holy grail as a stone brought to earth too early by "neutral angels," so called for refusing to take sides during the war in heaven.

IOWA POETRY PRIZE AND
EDWIN FORD PIPER POETRY AWARD WINNERS

1987
Elton Glaser, *Tropical Depressions*
Michael Pettit, *Cardinal Points*

1988
Bill Knott, *Outremer*
Mary Ruefle, *The Adamant*

1989
Conrad Hilberry, *Sorting the Smoke*
Terese Svoboda, *Laughing Africa*

1990
Philip Dacey, *Night Shift at the
    Crucifix Factory*
Lynda Hull, *Star Ledger*

1991
Greg Pape, *Sunflower Facing the Sun*
Walter Pavlich, *Running near the
    End of the World*

1992
Lola Haskins, *Hunger*
Katherine Soniat, *A Shared Life*

1993
Tom Andrews, *The Hemophiliac's
    Motorcycle*
Michael Heffernan, *Love's Answer*
John Wood, *In Primary Light*

1994
James McKean, *Tree of Heaven*
Bin Ramke, *Massacre of the
    Innocents*
Ed Roberson, *Voices Cast Out to Talk
    Us In*

1995
Ralph Burns, *Swamp Candles*
Maureen Seaton, *Furious Cooking*

1996
Pamela Alexander, *Inland*
Gary Gildner, *The Bunker in the
    Parsley Fields*
John Wood, *The Gates of the Elect
    Kingdom*

1997
Brendan Galvin, *Hotel Malabar*
Leslie Ullman, *Slow Work through
    Sand*

1998
Kathleen Peirce, *The Oval Hour*
Bin Ramke, *Wake*
Cole Swensen, *Try*

1999
Larissa Szporluk, *Isolato*
Liz Waldner, *A Point Is That Which
    Has No Part*

2000
Mary Leader, *The Penultimate Suitor*

2001
Joanna Goodman, *Trace of One*
Karen Volkman, *Spar*

2002
Lesle Lewis, *Small Boat*
Peter Jay Shippy, *Thieves' Latin*